Fun Foodie Friends

A COOKBOOK Where Fun is the First Ingredient

WRITTEN BY
Elaine Callahan
Joyce Kesler

ILLUSTRATED BY
Elaine Callahan

fun foodie friends

fun is the first ingredient™

Table of Contents

Food Head Fred Says

Let's Have Some Fun!

Hey, Kid Chefs, I'm Food Head Fred, and this is Food Head Fruita! We'll be your guides throughout the cookbook. Look for our fun food facts and helpful cooking tips and terms to help you enjoy creating yummy treats.

This cookbook is all about the food, the fun, and the friends you'll make—with your fruits and vegetables—as you create delicious food to share with the people you love.

As you go through this book, you'll learn not just how to cook, but the joy of making something with your own hands. You'll be able to spend time with your family and friends and enjoy the yummy food you've created.

We're here to help you have a great time in the kitchen and use your imagination to create new friends with your fruits and vegetables.

Plus, in addition to the recipes, there are fun activities in the back of the book for you to enjoy.

Now, let's have some cooking fun!

The Fun Fives to Understanding the Recipes

1 Prep Time and Serving – This will tell you how much time it will take for you to create this recipe and how many servings it will make.

2 Ingredients – All the ingredients you will need are listed here.

3 Directions – Follow the step-by-step directions listed here to create your recipe.

4 Tools – All the tools you will need are listed here.

5 Level of Difficulty – The Big Hands Helping symbols are used in each recipe to rate the amount of assistance a Kid Chef may require from an adult's helping hand.

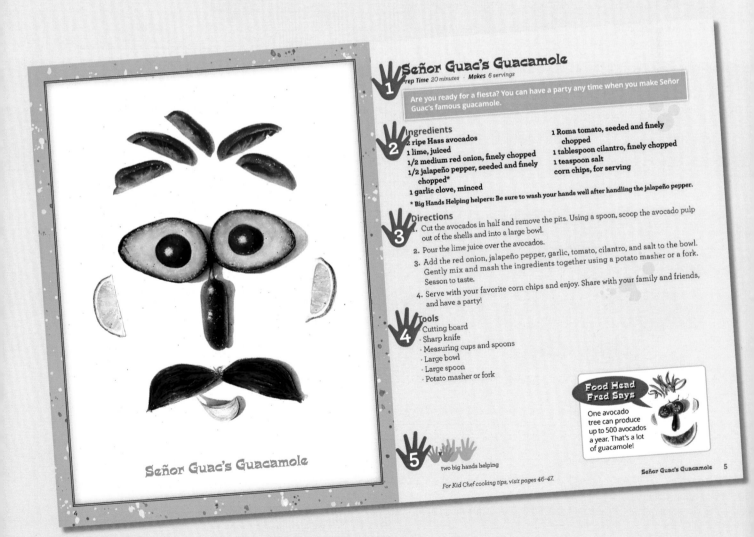

Señor Guac's Guacamole

Señor Guac's Guacamole

1 Prep Time *20 minutes* · **Makes** *6 servings*

Are you ready for a fiesta? You can have a party any time when you make Señor Guac's famous guacamole.

2 Ingredients

2 ripe Hass avocados
1 lime, juiced
1/2 medium red onion, finely chopped
1/2 jalapeño pepper, seeded and finely chopped*
1 garlic clove, minced

1 Roma tomato, seeded and finely chopped
1 tablespoon cilantro, finely chopped
1 teaspoon salt
corn chips, for serving

* Big Hands Helping helpers: Be sure to wash your hands well after handling the jalapeño pepper.

3 Directions

1. Cut the avocados in half and remove the pits. Using a spoon, scoop the avocado pulp out of the shells and into a large bowl.
2. Pour the lime juice over the avocados.
3. Add the red onion, jalapeño pepper, garlic, tomato, cilantro, and salt to the bowl. Gently mix and mash the ingredients together using a potato masher or a fork. Season to taste.
4. Serve with your favorite corn chips and enjoy. Share with your family and friends, and have a party!

4 Tools
- Cutting board
- Sharp knife
- Measuring cups and spoons
- Large bowl
- Large spoon
- Potato masher or fork

Food Head Fred Says

One avocado tree can produce up to 500 avocados a year. That's a lot of guacamole!

5 two big hands helping

For Kid Chef cooking tips, visit pages 46–47.

Señor Guac's Guacamole   5

Know What the Big Hands Helping Symbols Mean

When a Kid Chef is in the kitchen, there should always be a parent or an adult present. The Big Hands Helping  symbols that appear on each recipe give you an idea of the level of help your Kid Chef may need. These are only guidelines. You know your Kid Chef best, so please discuss the steps where they may need help as you review the recipes together.

kids' hands cooking

Kids' Hands Cooking
Recipes with this symbol do not require any cutting with sharp knives, boiling water, or a hot oven—just a watchful eye over the process.

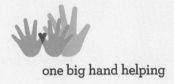

one big hand helping

One Big Hand Helping
Recipes with this symbol may have one or two steps that require using a sharp knife, a hot oven, microwave, the stove top, or a step that requires the use of the food processor or blender. One Big Hand may be needed to assist your Kid Chef to ensure that the steps are completed safely. You can make something really great with a little help from a big hand.

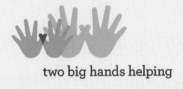

two big hands helping

Two Big Hands Helping
Two Big Hands are needed when boiling water or using other high temperature settings on the stove top or when multiple steps require using a sharp knife, a hot oven, a microwave, or the stove top. Recipes with this symbol require Two Big Hands Helping to step in and assist the Kid Chef so that their creations are completed safely and with confidence.

Señor Guac's Guacamole

Señor Guac's Guacamole

Prep Time *20 minutes* · **Makes** *6 servings*

Are you ready for a fiesta? You can have a party any time when you make Señor Guac's famous guacamole.

Ingredients

2 ripe Hass avocados

1 lime, juiced

1/2 medium red onion, finely chopped

1/2 jalapeño pepper, seeded and finely chopped*

1 garlic clove, minced

1 Roma tomato, seeded and finely chopped

1 tablespoon cilantro, finely chopped

1 teaspoon salt

corn chips, for serving

* **Big Hands Helping helpers:** Be sure to wash your hands well after handling the jalapeño pepper.

Directions

1. Cut the avocados in half and remove the pits. Using a spoon, scoop the avocado pulp out of the shells and into a large bowl.

2. Pour the lime juice over the avocados.

3. Add the red onion, jalapeño pepper, garlic, tomato, cilantro, and salt to the bowl. Gently mix and mash the ingredients together using a potato masher or a fork. Season to taste.

4. Serve with your favorite corn chips and enjoy. Share with your family and friends, and have a party!

Tools

· Cutting board
· Sharp knife
· Measuring cups and spoons
· Large bowl
· Large spoon
· Potato masher or fork

Food Head Fred Says

One avocado tree can produce up to 500 avocados a year. That's a lot of guacamole!

two big hands helping

For Kid Chef cooking tips, visit pages 46–47.

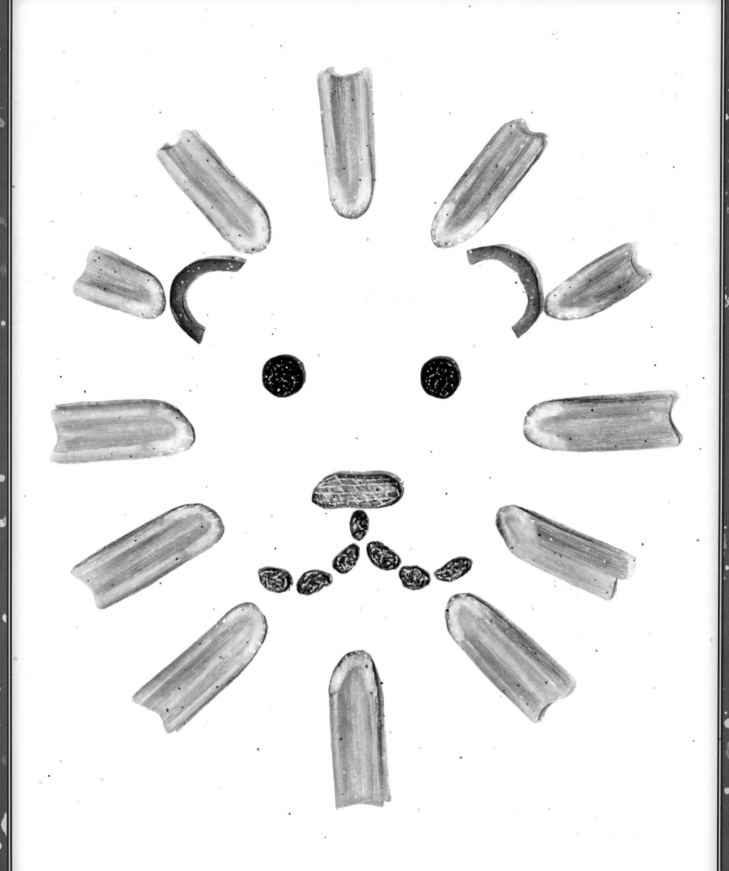

Leo Lion Celery Sliders

Leo Lion Celery Sliders

Prep Time *10 minutes* · **Makes** *6 servings*

Mix and match yummy fillings and toppings to make these Leo Lion Celery Sliders, and you'll be feeling like the king of the jungle. *Roooar!*

Ingredients

1 package of pre-cut, pre-washed celery stalks

fillings, such as cream cheese*, peanut butter**, and pimento cheese* (Use one OR all of these fillings to create a variety of sliders.)

toppings, such as raisins, cranberries, dried cherries, peanuts**, and cut red peppers (Use one OR all of these toppings to create a variety of sliders.)

* For dairy free, substitute with dairy-free cream cheese.
** Do not use if you have a peanut allergy.

Directions

1. Use a spreader or butter knife to fill the inside of each of the stalks with your choice of filling.

2. Add dried fruit, peanuts, or other toppings to decorate the top. Try yummy combinations such as cream cheese and dried cherries, peanut butter and raisins, or peanuts and pimento cheese. Or use your imagination to make up your own fun flavors!

3. Slide the stalks on a plate and enjoy.

Tools

· Spreader or butter knife
· Plate

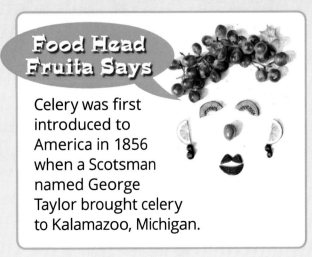

Food Head Fruita Says

Celery was first introduced to America in 1856 when a Scotsman named George Taylor brought celery to Kalamazoo, Michigan.

kids' hands cooking

For Kid Chef cooking tips, visit pages 46–47.

America the Fruitiful
Jell-O-bration

America the Fruitiful Jell-O-bration

Prep Time 30 minutes · *Chill Time* 2–3 hours · *Makes* 8 servings

Celebrate fun with the red, white, and blue. Making this recipe will turn your celebration into a Jell-O-bration!

Ingredients

1 box of strawberry or cherry Jell-O
1 container whipped topping*
1/2 cup blueberries

1–2 cups cherries to allow plenty for decoration (Note: Leave the stems on to let people know there are pits inside!)

* For dairy free, substitute with dairy-free whipped topping.

Directions

1. Follow the directions on the Jell-O box for making Jell-O. Ask for help from your Big Hands Helping helper when handling the boiling water.

2. Pour the Jell-O into an 8″ x 8″ pan, and refrigerate until it is well chilled and set, at least 2–3 hours.

3. Once it is well chilled, cover the Jell-O with a thick layer of whipped topping. Usually, about 1 cup is needed, but make it as thick as you like.

4. Place the blueberries in a rectangle in one corner, like the stars on the American flag. Then, place the cherries in rows, like the red stripes on the flag.

5. Place the "flag" back in the refrigerator to chill for an additional 15–20 minutes.

6. Cut the "flag" into squares for serving. Place any extra blueberries and cherries into serving bowls for your family and friends to add to their piece of the flag.

Tools

- Bowl
- Measuring cup
- Large spoon
- Potholder
- 8″ x 8″ pan
- Spatula or spreader

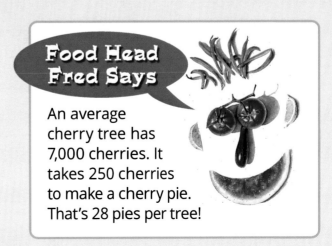

Food Head Fred Says

An average cherry tree has 7,000 cherries. It takes 250 cherries to make a cherry pie. That's 28 pies per tree!

two big hands helping

For Kid Chef cooking tips, visit pages 46–47.

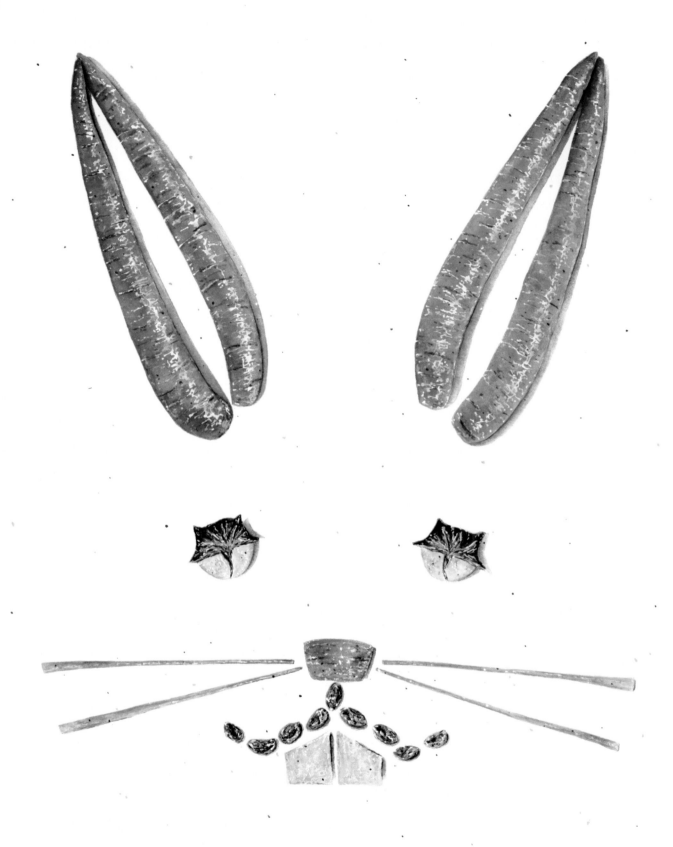

Rodney Rabbit's Secret Carrot Salad

Rodney Rabbit's Secret Carrot Salad

Prep Time *15 minutes* · **Chill Time** *1 hour* · **Makes** *8 servings*

> Wonder why Rodney Rabbit can see and hear so well? It must be the carrots in his Secret Carrot Salad. Shh, now the secret is out.

Ingredients

4 cups bagged, pre-shredded carrots
1 1/4 cups raisins (dark or golden)
1/2 cup small chunks of fresh pineapple
    or 10.5 oz. can of well-drained pineapple
    chunks

1/3 cup mayonnaise*
1 tablespoon sugar
3 tablespoons milk**

* For egg free, substitute with egg-free mayonnaise.
** For dairy free, substitute with dairy-free milk.

Directions

1. Mix the carrots, raisins, and pineapple in a large bowl.
2. In a small bowl, combine the mayonnaise, sugar, and milk until creamy.
3. Pour the dressing mixture over the carrots, raisins, and pineapple.
4. Mix well to coat.
5. Cover and chill for an hour or more.

Tools

· Measuring cups and spoons
· 2 bowls—one large, one small
· Can opener
· Strainer (for pineapple)
· Mixing spoon

Food Head Fruita Says

Carrots first came in the colors purple, red, white, and yellow, but never orange. Sixteenth-century Dutch carrot growers crossbred pale yellow carrots with red ones to create orange carrots in honor of the House of Orange, the Dutch Royal Family.

one big hand helping

For Kid Chef cooking tips, visit pages 46–47.

Fruitiful Fruit Kabobs

Fruitiful Fruit Kabobs

Prep Time *15 minutes* · **Makes** *6 servings*

> Fruitiful Fruit Kabobs are fun to make and sweet to eat! Use a rainbow of different fruits to add more color and flavor to your creations!

Ingredients*

1 cup strawberries

1 cup orange sections

1 cup pre-cut cantaloupe

1/2 cup kiwi slices

1/2 cup blueberries

1/2 cup purple grapes

8″ bamboo skewers

* Use seasonal and local organic fruits if possible for the best flavor.

Directions

1. Wash the fruit and cut the strawberries in half.

2. Take one strawberry and pierce the center of it with a bamboo skewer. Add an orange section, then a piece of cantaloupe, and after that, a piece of kiwi. Add two blueberries and finally two purple grapes until the skewer is full.

3. Repeat step 2 to make multiple kabobs. Or, mix up the color and fruits on hand to make your own colorful creation. Serve.

Tools

- Cutting board
- Sharp knife
- Measuring cups
- Small bowls
- 8″ bamboo skewers

Food Head Fred Says

One kiwi fruit has more fiber than a bowl of corn flakes.

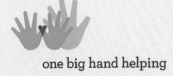

one big hand helping

Hoot-Hoot
Smashed-Mashed Potatoes

Hoot-Hoot Smashed-Mashed Potatoes

Prep Time *15 minutes* · ***Cook Time*** *15 minutes* · ***Makes*** *6 servings*

> **Hoot-Hoot is wise about his Smashed-Mashed Potatoes. He loves to smash them *and* mash them to make them extra delicious. You will, too!**

Ingredients

1 1/2 lbs. Yukon Gold potatoes

1/2 cup milk*

1 tablespoon butter**

salt & pepper

2 scallions, chopped or cut with kitchen scissors

* For dairy free, substitute with dairy-free milk, or use chicken broth.

** For dairy free, substitute with dairy-free spread.

Directions

1. Wash the potatoes, leaving the skins on. Cut into quarters.

2. Place the potatoes in a large pot. Cover with water and bring to a boil. After the potatoes boil, put the lid on the pot, turn down the heat, and let simmer for about 15 minutes until tender.

3. When the potatoes feel almost tender when pricked with a fork, warm up the milk in the microwave or in a saucepan on the stove.

4. Use pot holders to lift the pot and drain the potatoes well in a strainer over the sink.

5. Pour the drained potatoes into a bowl, and add the butter.

6. Take the potato masher and smash the potatoes just enough so that there aren't any big chunks left. Don't overdo it.

7. Add the warm milk a little at a time, smashing after each addition. Season with salt and pepper. Sprinkle chopped scallions over the top.

Tools

· Cutting board
· Sharp knife
· Measuring cup
· Large pot with a lid
· Pot holders
· Strainer
· Bowl
· Potato masher

two big hands helping

Food Head Fruita Says

The potato originally came from the Andes Mountains in South America.

For Kid Chef cooking tips, visit pages 46–47.

Wonderful Wendy's Watermelon Pops

Wonderful Wendy's Watermelon Pops

Prep Time 15 minutes · *Chill Time* 10 hours or overnight · *Makes* 8 servings

Wonderful Wendy's Watermelon Pops are perfect for a hot summer day. They will cool you off and are wonderfully easy-breezy to make!

Ingredients

2 cups seedless watermelon, cubed

1 lime, juiced

1/2 cup raspberries

1 tablespoon sugar

Directions

1. Place cubed watermelon in the blender.

2. Pour the lime juice in the blender.

3. Add raspberries and sugar, and blend until smooth.

4. Pour mixture into ice pop molds and insert handles. Freeze until firm, several hours or overnight. Enjoy within 1 week of creating.

Tools

· Cutting board
· Sharp knife
· Measuring cups and spoons
· Blender
· Ice pop molds

Food Head Fred Says

The first recorded watermelon harvest was nearly 5,000 years ago in Egypt.

one big hand helping

For Kid Chef cooking tips, visit pages 46-47.

Monkey Magic Banana Ice Cream

Monkey Magic Banana Ice Cream

Prep Time *5 minutes* · **Chill Time** *2 hours* · **Makes** *2 servings*

No monkeying around here. This Monkey Magic Banana Ice Cream will have you going bananas for more!

Ingredients

2 ripe peeled bananas, cut into chunks

1 teaspoon vanilla extract

2–4 tablespoons milk* or fruit juice

ice cream cones**

chocolate sauce

blueberries or strawberries (optional)

* For dairy free, substitute with dairy-free milk.

** For gluten free, substitute with gluten-free ice cream cones.

Directions

1. Place banana chunks in a freezer bag or container.

2. Freeze until solid, about 2 hours.

3. Put the frozen banana into a food processor, and add the vanilla and a few tablespoons of milk or juice.

4. Process until you have a "soft serve" texture, adding milk or juice in small amounts if needed.

5. Serve in a cone or in ice cream dishes with chocolate sauce.

6. For a special treat, add strawberries or blueberries to the frozen banana when processing.

Tools

- Cutting board
- Small knife
- Measuring spoons
- Freezer bag or freezer container
- Food processor

Food Head Fruita Says

A row of bananas is called a "hand," while a single banana is called a "finger."

one big hand helping

For Kid Chef cooking tips, visit pages 46–47.

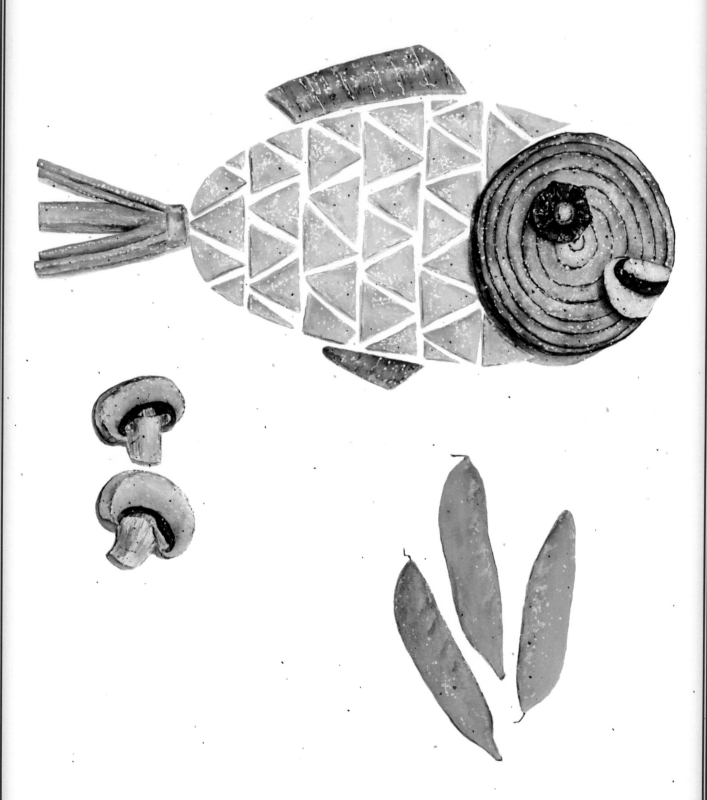

Splish-Splash Vegetable Stir Fry

Splish-Splash Vegetable Stir Fry

Prep Time *20 minutes* · **Cook Time** *10 minutes* · **Makes** *4 servings*

Have an ocean full of veggies and want to know what to do with them? Create Splish-Splash Vegetable Stir Fry. You will be swimming in flavor!

Ingredients

2 teaspoons peanut oil*

2–3 stalks of celery, cut on the diagonal into 1/2-inch pieces

1/2 cup shredded carrot

1/2 small onion, chopped

2 teaspoons fresh ginger, minced

1 clove garlic, minced

1/2 cup mushroom slices

1/2 cup snap peas

1/2 teaspoon toasted sesame oil

1/4 teaspoon red pepper flakes (optional)

1 tablespoon soy sauce**†

salt & pepper

* For peanut free, substitute with peanut-free oil.
** For gluten free, substitute with gluten-free soy sauce.
† For soy free, substitute with soy-free soy sauce.

Directions

1. Heat a large skillet or wok over high heat and add peanut oil.

2. Add the celery, carrots, and onion. Cook, stirring, until onion is just translucent.

3. Add the ginger and garlic. Cook, stirring, for about 30 seconds.

4. Add the mushrooms and snap peas and cook, stirring, until the peas are bright green and the mushrooms are tender.

5. Drizzle in the sesame oil and stir. Add the red pepper flakes, if using.

6. Add the soy sauce and stir to coat, then cook for 1 minute.

7. Add salt and pepper to taste.

Tools

· Cutting board
· Sharp knife
· Measuring cups and measuring spoons
· Small bowls
· Potholder
· 10" skillet or wok

two big hands helping

Food Head Fred Says

Onions can predict the severity of winter. Thin skins mean a mild winter is coming, while thick skins indicate a rough winter ahead.

For Kid Chef cooking tips, visit pages 46–47.

Señor Sammy's Salsa

Señor Sammy's Salsa

Prep Time *15 minutes* · **Makes** *6 servings*

Señor Sammy is Señor Guac's best friend. They enjoy making this salsa and Señor Guac's Guacamole together for an extra special treat. Friends enjoying good food together is the best!

Ingredients

4 Roma tomatoes, finely chopped

1 lime, juiced

1/2 jalapeño pepper, seeded and finely chopped*

1/2 medium green pepper, seeded and finely chopped

1/2 medium red onion, finely chopped

1 garlic clove, minced

1 tablespoon cilantro, chopped

1 teaspoon salt

1/2 teaspoon ground cumin

corn chips, for serving

* Big Hands Helping helpers: Be sure to wash your hands well after handling the jalapeño pepper.

Directions

1. Add the chopped tomatoes to a large bowl.

2. Add the remaining ingredients (except the corn chips) to the tomatoes, and mix together well with a spoon. Season to taste.

3. Cover with plastic wrap, and place in the refrigerator until ready to serve.

4. Serve with your favorite corn chips and enjoy. Share with your family and friends, and have a party!

Tools

· Cutting board
· Sharp knife
· Measuring cups and spoons
· Large bowl
· Large spoon

Food Head Fruita Says

Tomatoes are thought to have originated in Peru. The name tomato comes from the Aztec word *xitomatl*, which means "plump thing with a navel."

two big hands helping

For Kid Chef cooking tips, visit pages 46-47.

Prince Peacock's Roasted Asparagus

Prince Peacock's Roasted Asparagus

Prep Time *15 minutes* · **Cook Time** *15 minutes* · **Makes** *8 servings*

Prince Peacock's Roasted Asparagus gets the royal treatment with a splash of lemon juice right before serving. Perfect for a prince or princess!

Ingredients

1 bunch of asparagus, large
2 tablespoons olive oil
1 teaspoon sea salt

1/2 teaspoon pepper
1/4 of a lemon

Directions

1. Pre-heat oven to 425 degrees.

2. After washing and drying asparagus, take a handful of the asparagus stems and bend them until the bottom snaps off. That will be about 1/3 of the asparagus stem, which can be discarded. Do this to all the stems.

3. Cover the top of a cookie sheet with aluminum foil. This will make cleanup easier!

4. Place asparagus stems on the sheet in a single layer. Lightly drizzle the olive oil over all of them. Sprinkle with sea salt and pepper.

5. Put in oven and cook for 12–15 minutes, until the asparagus is tender.

6. Place roasted asparagus stems on a serving platter and squeeze the lemon over them.

Tools

- Measuring spoons
- Aluminum foil
- Cookie sheet
- Serving platter
- Oven mitts
- Hot pad

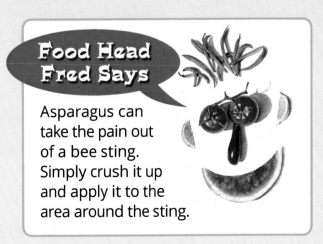

Food Head Fred Says

Asparagus can take the pain out of a bee sting. Simply crush it up and apply it to the area around the sting.

two big hands helping

For Kid Chef cooking tips, visit pages 46–47.

QT Caterpillar's
Cucumber Watermelon Feta Salad

QT Caterpillar's Cucumber Watermelon Feta Salad

Prep Time *15 minutes* · ***Makes*** *4 servings*

> What's cool as a cucumber, sweet as a watermelon, and cute as a caterpillar with just a touch of mint? It's QT Caterpillar's Cucumber Watermelon Feta Salad!

Ingredients

2 cups watermelon cubes, bite size

1 cucumber (English seedless), sliced or cubed

5 mint leaves, minced or cut in a chiffonade (see page 48)

1 tablespoon lime juice

1 tablespoon olive oil

black pepper

1/2 cup crumbled Feta cheese*

* For dairy free, have your Big Hands Helping helper determine if you can eat Feta cheese.

Directions

1. Toss the watermelon, cucumbers, and half of the mint leaves in a large bowl.

2. Season with lime juice and olive oil.

3. Grind some fresh black pepper in and toss again.

4. Sprinkle with the Feta cheese and remaining mint leaves.

Tools

- Cutting board
- Sharp knife
- Large bowl
- Spoon
- Measuring cups and measuring spoons

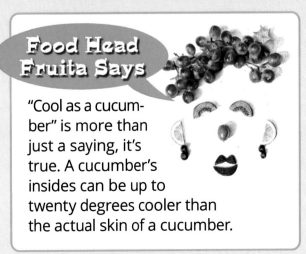

Food Head Fruita Says

"Cool as a cucumber" is more than just a saying, it's true. A cucumber's insides can be up to twenty degrees cooler than the actual skin of a cucumber.

one big hand helping

Rockin' Rooster's Stuffed Burritos

Rockin' Rooster's Stuffed Burritos

Prep Time 25 minutes · *Cook Time 35 minutes* · *Makes 4 servings*

Rockin' Rooster's Stuffed Burritos are so stuffed with deliciousness, you will be crowing about them to everyone you know!

Ingredients

2 teaspoons olive oil
1 medium onion, chopped
1/2 cup celery, chopped
2 cloves garlic, minced
2 teaspoons ground cumin
2 teaspoons ground coriander
1 tablespoon chili powder
1 14.5 oz. can diced tomatoes with juice

1 16 oz. can black beans, drained and rinsed
1/2 cup water
1 cup cooked rice
8 8" tortillas*
1 cup shredded cheddar cheese**
salt

* For gluten free, substitute with gluten-free tortillas.
** For dairy free, substitute with dairy-free cheese.

Directions

1. Heat the oil in a large skillet. Add the onion and celery, and cook until the onion is translucent.
2. Add the garlic and cook for 1 minute.
3. Add the cumin, coriander, and chili powder. Stir for 30 seconds.
4. Add the canned tomatoes with the juice, black beans, water, and rice. Salt to taste. Bring to a simmer, and simmer for 15 minutes.
5. Place skillet on a hot pad.
6. Fill each tortilla with a scoop of the mixture, and place each one, fold down, in the baking dish, nestling them close together.
7. Sprinkle the cheese on top of the burritos.
8. Cover the dish with aluminum foil, shiny side in, and bake at 375 degrees for 30 minutes. Remove the foil and bake another 5 minutes to brown the cheese.

Tools

- Cutting board
- Sharp knife
- Measuring cups and spoons
- Strainer
- Grater
- 10" skillet
- Large spoon
- Hot pad
- 9" x 13" baking dish
- Aluminum foil
- Oven mitts

Food Head Fred Says

Garlic is so old that six bulbs of it were discovered in the tomb of the Egyptian pharaoh Tutankhamun. Now that's old!

two big hands helping

For Kid Chef cooking tips, visit pages 46–47.

Hop Hoppin' Cucumber Sandwiches

Hop Hoppin' Cucumber Sandwiches

Prep Time *10 minutes* · ***Makes*** *4 servings*

Hop Hoppin' Cucumber Sandwiches are perfect when you need a quick snack. They will have you saying "ribbit" in two hops and a jump!

Ingredients

1 cucumber

favorite hummus spread

Directions

1. Peel cucumber with a peeler.
2. To create a decorative ribbing pattern on the cucumber, take a fork and gently press against the cucumber from top to bottom, repeating until the pattern is around the entire cucumber. (Optional.)
3. Cut the cucumber into round slices about 1/4-inch wide.
4. Put a little bit of hummus on one cucumber slice. Top with another cucumber slice.
5. Place the sandwiches on a plate and enjoy.

Tools

- Peeler
- Cutting board
- Fork
- Sharp knife
- Plate

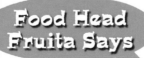

Food Head Fruita Says

A cucumber can be a great snack any time because it relieves the feeling of hunger in our minds, and it is better for you than a candy bar or soda!

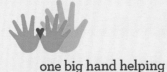

one big hand helping

For Kid Chef cooking tips, visit pages 46–47.

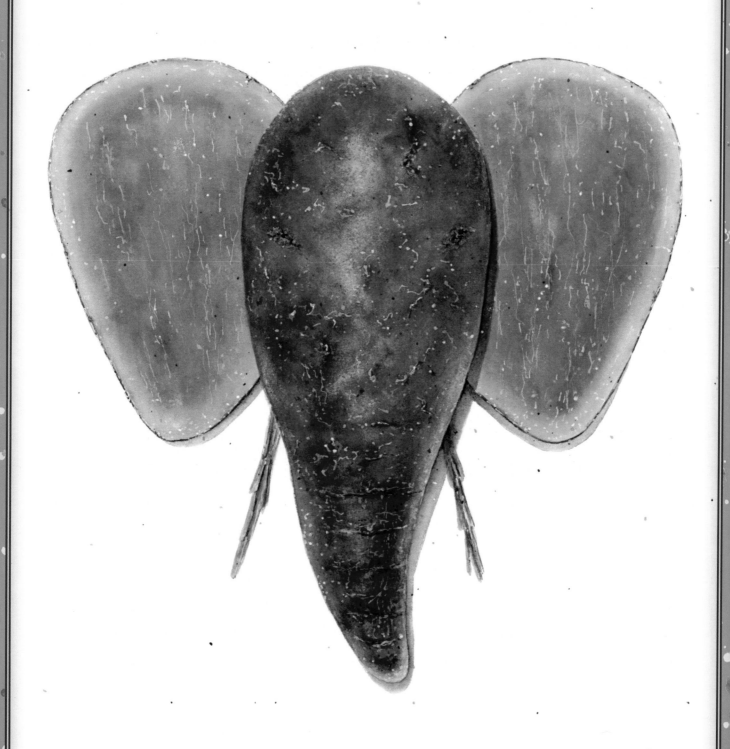

Sweet Ela's
Savory Sweet Potato Wedges

Sweet Ela's Savory Sweet Potato Wedges

***Prep Time** 10 minutes · **Cook Time** 40 minutes · **Makes** 4 servings*

> Sweet Ela enjoys these Savory Sweet Potato Wedges. Sometimes she likes to spice things up with a sprinkle of paprika.

Ingredients

2 large sweet potatoes, scrubbed clean
1 tablespoon extra virgin olive oil

2 tablespoons minced fresh rosemary
salt & pepper

Directions

1. Pre-heat oven to 400 degrees.

2. Cut each sweet potato in half. Take each half and place cut side down on the cutting board. Cut the halves in half again to make quarters, then cut each quarter in half to make wedges.

3. Place the wedges in the bowl, and pour in the olive oil. Toss to make sure the pieces are well coated.

4. Sprinkle the rosemary evenly over the potatoes.

5. Add the salt and pepper to taste.

6. Stir to coat well.

7. Place the wedges on the baking sheet and cook for 35–40 minutes.

8. Roast until they are browned and tender, turning once halfway through the cooking time.

Tools

- Cutting board
- Sharp knife
- Measuring spoons
- Large bowl
- Baking sheet
- Oven mitts
- Hot pad

two big hands helping

Food Head Fred Says

Sweet potatoes are a Native American plant that kept the early settlers nourished.

Berry Blue Blueberry Pie

Berry Blue Blueberry Pie

Prep Time *15 minutes* · **Chill Time** *2 hours* · **Makes** *6 servings*

There are plenty of blueberries to enjoy in Berry Blue Blueberry Pie. In fact, there are five whole cups of them!

Ingredients

5 cups fresh blueberries, rinsed

1/2 cup turbinado sugar
  OR 3/4 cup regular sugar

3 tablespoons cornstarch

1/8 teaspoon salt

1/4 cup water

1 tablespoon butter

1 tablespoon lemon juice

1 baked 9" pie shell*

whipped cream, ice cream, or yogurt**

* For gluten free, substitute with a gluten-free pie shell.
** For dairy free, substitute with dairy-free whipped cream, ice cream, or yogurt.

Directions

1. Place 2 cups of the rinsed blueberries in a saucepan with the sugar, cornstarch, salt, and water. Gently stir to combine.

2. Cook over medium heat until the mixture boils and thickens, about 3–4 minutes. Stir occasionally to keep the mixture from sticking to the bottom.

3. Remove from the heat. Place the saucepan on a hot pad and lightly mash the blueberry mixture. There should still be some whole blueberries in the mixture.

4. Add the butter and lemon juice, and stir to combine. Let sit.

5. Pour the remaining 3 cups of fresh blueberries into the pie shell. Pour the cooked blueberry mixture over the fresh berries. Gently shake the pie plate to move the mixture around.

6. Chill at least 2 hours or until set.

7. Serve with your favorite topping: whipped cream, ice cream, or yogurt.

Tools

- 9" pie plate
- Measuring cup and spoons
- Saucepan
- Spoon
- Potholder
- Hot pad
- Potato masher

one big hand helping

Food Head Fruita Says

If all the blueberries grown in North America in one year were spread out in a single layer, they would cover a four-lane highway that stretched from New York to Chicago.

For Kid Chef cooking tips, visit pages 46–47.

Bow-Wow Lettuce Wraps and Dip

Bow-Wow Lettuce Wraps and Dip

Prep Time 15 minutes · *Chill Time* 10 minutes · *Makes* 4 servings

Is your stomach growling like a dog? Try these Bow-Wow Lettuce Wraps, and soon you will be one happy pup.

Ingredients

Dipping Sauce
1/2 of an English cucumber
1/2 cup plain yogurt*
2 tablespoons cilantro, minced
2 teaspoons green onions, white part only, chopped
1/4 teaspoon ground coriander
1/4 teaspoon ground cumin

* For dairy free, substitute with dairy-free yogurt.

Wrap
Iceberg, Bibb, or Romaine lettuce leaves washed and dried well
1 large carrot, cut into 2-inch strips
1 avocado, cut into slices
2 celery ribs, cut into thin 2-inch strips
1/2 of a red pepper cut into thin strips

Directions

1. Peel the cucumber. Seed the cucumber by cutting it in half lengthwise and then in half again lengthwise into quarters. Use a teaspoon to scrape down the center, removing all of the seeds.

2. Cut the cucumber into small bits.

3. Combine the cucumber and the rest of the dipping sauce ingredients in a bowl and mix well.

4. Place sauce in the refrigerator to chill while you prepare the lettuce wrap ingredients.

5. Place the lettuce leaves in a serving bowl or on a plate.

6. Arrange the carrots, avocado, celery, and red pepper on another serving plate.

7. Remove the dipping sauce from the refrigerator.

8. To create the wraps, take a lettuce leaf and place a few pieces of each of the vegetable fillings in the middle. Roll up and dip into the sauce.

Tools

- Cutting board
- Peeler
- Sharp knife
- Measuring cup and spoons
- Bowl
- Spoon
- Serving bowl
- Serving plates

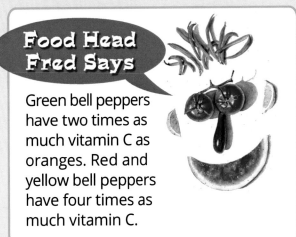

Food Head Fred Says

Green bell peppers have two times as much vitamin C as oranges. Red and yellow bell peppers have four times as much vitamin C.

one big hand helping

For Kid Chef cooking tips, visit pages 46–47.

Peary Penguin's
Pear and Cranberry Crisp

Peary Penguin's Pear and Cranberry Crisp

Prep Time 15 minutes · *Cook Time* 45 minutes · *Makes* 6–8 servings

> Making Peary Penguin's Pear and Cranberry Crisp will warm your heart and tummy. And, if you're like Peary, you will enjoy it cold the next day.

Ingredients

Filling
3/4 cup dried cranberries
4 Bartlett pears (2 lbs.)
1/3 cup honey
3 tablespoons cornstarch
1 tablespoon lemon juice
1/2 teaspoon cinnamon
1/8 teaspoon nutmeg

Topping
1 cup old-fashioned oats*
1/4 cup coconut flour
1/2 cup brown sugar
pinch of salt
4 tablespoons butter, cut into small bits
4 tablespoons any plain yogurt**
vanilla ice cream or whipped topping**

* For gluten free, substitute with gluten-free oats.
** For dairy free, substitute with dairy-free yogurt, vanilla ice cream, or whipped topping.

Directions

1. Pre-heat oven to 350 degrees.
2. In a small bowl, pour very hot water over the dried cranberries to plump them up; let them sit while you peel, core, and dice the pears. Drain the cranberries.
3. Place the cranberries and the rest of the filling ingredients in a 9"x 9" baking dish, and stir to combine.
4. In a bowl, mix all the topping ingredients together with a fork. Stir until all the flour is incorporated and the mix barely clings together in lumps.
5. Drop the topping mixture in clumps all over the top of the filling, then use your fingers to spread it out evenly.
6. Bake for 45 minutes, or until the topping is brown and the filling is bubbling around the edge. Let rest on a hot pad for 10 minutes. Serve warm with ice cream or whipped topping.

Tools

- 2 bowls
- Cutting board
- Sharp knife
- Peeler
- Measuring cups and spoons
- 9" x 9" baking dish
- Spoon
- Fork
- Oven mitts
- Hot pad

Food Head Fruita Says

Pear wood is perfect for kitchen utensils because it doesn't leach color, have an odor, warp, or splinter.

one big hand helping

For Kid Chef cooking tips, visit pages 46–47.

Lady Gala's Overnight Applesauce

Lady Gala's Overnight Applesauce

Prep Time 20 minutes · *Cook Time* 8–10 hours · *Makes* 6 cups

Lady Gala takes a snooze while the apples cook for her Overnight Applesauce. The mornings seem brighter when there is the aroma of sweet apples in the air.

Ingredients

8–10 large cooking apples, such as McIntosh, Honey Crisp, or Gala

1/2 cup apple cider

1 teaspoon cinnamon

1/2 cup sugar, granulated or brown*

* Brown sugar makes the applesauce a richer dark color.

Directions

1. Peel, core, and cut each apple into 8 large chunks.

2. Put all the ingredients into the slow cooker. It should be about 3/4 full. The apples will cook down.

3. Cover and cook on low for 8–10 hours or for 3–4 hours on high.

4. Depending on your personal preference for consistency, mash the apples with a potato masher for a chunky sauce, or put small batches of the sauce into a food processor or blender to create a smoother texture.

5. The sauce will keep for several days in the refrigerator, or you can freeze the sauce in small batches.

Tools

- Cutting board
- Paring knife
- Measuring cup and spoons
- Peeler
- Slow cooker or crockpot
- Potato masher
- Potholder
- Food processor/blender
- Large spoon

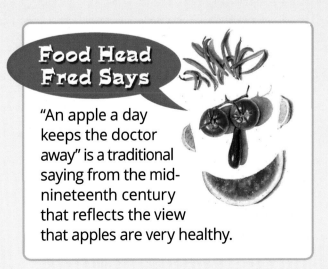

Food Head Fred Says

"An apple a day keeps the doctor away" is a traditional saying from the mid-nineteenth century that reflects the view that apples are very healthy.

one big hand helping

For Kid Chef cooking tips, visit pages 46–47.

Princess Vivien's Very Vegetable Soup

Princess Vivien's Very Vegetable Soup

Prep Time 15 minutes · *Cook Time* 45 minutes · *Makes* 6 servings

> No peas for Princess Vivien. Her Very Vegetable Soup is filled with bright colored, flavorful vegetables. Is it the carrots that keep her hair so bright and vivid?

Ingredients

1 tablespoon olive oil
1 leek, white part only, chopped
1 tablespoon garlic, minced
1 carrot, cut into rounds
3 new potatoes, peeled, and cut in a large dice
1 cup green beans, broken into 1-inch pieces

4 cups vegetable broth
2 medium tomatoes peeled, seeded, and chopped
2 ears of corn, kernels removed (optional)
2 teaspoons lemon juice
1 tablespoon fresh parsley, chopped
kosher salt and pepper

Directions

1. Heat the olive oil in large, heavy-bottomed stockpot over medium-low heat. Add the leek, garlic, and a pinch of salt. Stir until they are just soft, about 7–8 minutes.

2. Add the carrot, potatoes, and green beans, and continue to cook for 4–5 more minutes, stirring occasionally.

3. Add the vegetable broth, increase the heat to high, and bring to a simmer.

4. Add the tomatoes, corn kernels (if using), and pepper to taste.

5. Reduce the heat to low, cover, and cook until the vegetables are fork tender, approximately 25–30 minutes.

6. Remove from the heat, set the pot on a hot pad, and add the lemon juice and parsley.

7. Season to taste with the salt.

8. Spoon into bowls.

Tools

- Cutting board
- Sharp knife
- Measuring cups and spoons
- Stockpot
- Large spoon
- Fork
- Potholder
- Hot pad

two big hands helping

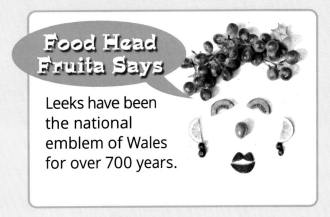

Food Head Fruita Says

Leeks have been the national emblem of Wales for over 700 years.

For Kid Chef cooking tips, visit pages 46–47.

Lemony Dragonslice Lemonade

Lemony Dragonslice Lemonade

Prep Time *15 minutes* · **Chill Time** *35 minutes* · **Makes** *8 servings*

> Dragonslice enjoys his Lemony Lemonade. It has a little bit of sugar and is long on lemony flavor, just the way he likes it.

Ingredients

1 cup water

1 cup sugar

1 cup fresh lemon juice (from 8–10 lemons)

5 cups cold water

6 thin lemon slices

ice cubes

Directions

1. Combine the 1 cup of water and the 1 cup of sugar in a half-gallon pitcher. Stir to incorporate the sugar. Let sit.

2. Roll the lemons on the cutting board to help release their juice.

3. Give the sugar water another stir to make sure that the sugar is dissolved.

4. Cut the lemons in half and place a strainer over a 2-cup liquid measuring cup.

5. Squeeze or use a reamer to juice the lemons over the strainer.

6. Give the sugar water another stir, and then add the lemon juice to the pitcher. Stir to combine.

7. Add the 5 cups of cold water and the lemon slices. Stir.

8. Put the pitcher in the refrigerator to chill for 35 minutes.

9. Pour the lemonade into tall glasses filled with ice cubes and enjoy!

Tools

· Cutting board
· Sharp knife
· Measuring cups
· Spoon
· Strainer
· Reamer
· Pitcher
· Tall glasses

Food Head Fred Says

Lemon trees bloom throughout the year. In that time, an average commercial tree yields about 1,500 lemons.

one big hand helping

For Kid Chef cooking tips, visit pages 46–47.

COOKING TIPS FOR KID CHEFS

Food Head Fred Says

Hey, Kid Chef, Want a Food Head Fred High Five? Complete the List Start to Finish!

First things first. All good chefs begin with the basics and get themselves organized.

1 Choose and Review the Recipe

- Read the recipe from start to finish, reviewing each step. If you don't understand something, now is the time to ask for help.

- Check the Big Hands Helping symbol to see if you should ask for a little help from an adult—a big hand. ✋

- Do you have a food allergy or food intolerance? Carefully read the ingredients to make sure it is safe for you to eat.

- Check the list of ingredients. Do you have everything on the list and in the quantities needed?

- Check the list of tools necessary to complete the recipe. Are they out and ready?

2 Safety Counts—Protect Yourself and Your Kitchen

- Make sure your apron is tied securely.

- Only use sharp equipment with adult permission and supervision.

- Place your oven mitts and potholders in a handy spot. *Always* use oven mitts or potholders when taking anything from the oven, microwave, or stove. Remember to ask for help from big hands  when removing items from the oven and microwave, too.

- Place hot pads on the counter tops so you have a safe place to put hot items from the oven, microwave, or stove.

- Secure your cutting boards. Place your cutting boards on a dish towel or other non-slick surface so they do not slip and slide when you are cutting and chopping.

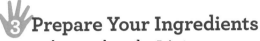

3 Prepare Your Ingredients

- Wash your hands. It's important for safe food preparation. Scrub your hands well for 20 seconds with warm soapy water, then rinse well and dry.

- We recommend using organic fruits and vegetables whenever possible in these recipes.

- Make sure all your vegetables and fruits are washed, rinsed, and ready before using them. A good way to clean your fruit and vegetables is to dunk them into a bowl of three cups cold water mixed with one cup of white vinegar. Swish the fruits and vegetables around, and then rinse them in cool water.

- Measure out all of your ingredients.

4 Let's Get Cooking

- Pre-heat the oven if needed.

- Complete all the tasks in each step of the recipe before beginning the next step.

- Before you serve your food, taste test your recipe with a clean spoon. It's the best way to tell if you have a good mix of food and seasonings.

5 Clean Up Counts

- Rinse your tools and put the appropriate ones in the dishwasher.

- Hand wash the tools that do not fit in the dishwasher.

- Put away unused ingredients in their proper places.

- Wipe off the counter tops, stove top, and microwave.

Did you complete all five steps? Food Head Fred says you deserve a high five! Way to go!

Give your Big Hands Helping helper a high five and enjoy your creation. Don't forget to share with your family and friends.

Want to learn more about the recipes and alternative ingredients? Visit funfoodiefriends.com.

Cooking Terms for Kid Chefs

Boil: To cook food in steadily bubbling water that has reached 212°F. Remember, liquid this hot will burn you, so be very careful and always use a potholder to handle hot items.

Chiffonade: French for "made of rags." It is a fancy term for cutting leaf herbs and lettuce into thin strips. Stack the leaves three or four high and, starting at the stem end, roll them into a tube. Then cut the tube into thin slices and shake out the slices, or "little rags," into strips.

Chill: To place food in the refrigerator to get cold or set.

Chop: To cut food into rough pieces, about 1/4 inch or larger.

Dice: A precise cut of equal proportions or size. This is so the food cooks evenly, and also gives the dish a pleasant appearance.

Drizzle: To pour a liquid such as melted chocolate, olive oil, or powdered sugar icing back and forth over food in a thin stream.

Dust: To lightly coat a food with dry ingredients, such as flour or powdered sugar. This can be done before or after cooking.

Freeze: To place food in the freezer until solid.

Grind: To cut food into tiny pieces using a food grinder or food processor.

Mash: To press, beat, or smash food to make a smooth mixture by removing all the lumps. You can mash with a potato masher, fork, potato ricer, or food processor.

Mince: To cut food into fine pieces, about 1/8 inch or smaller.

Mix: To use a spoon, spatula, fork, electric mixer, or food processor to combine all the ingredients, making sure that everything is well incorporated. It can get messy, but it should all stay in the bowl.

Pre-cut: Food that you can buy at the grocery store that's cut and ready to eat.

Pre-heat: To bring an oven, grill, or pan up to temperature before using it.

Prep or Prep Time: The process and the time it takes to prepare all the ingredients, including measuring and cutting the food.

Process: To prepare food in a food processor.

Simmer: To cook something just below the boiling point, when the bubbles slowly come to the surface. A slow simmer is often used with tomato sauces so that they do not burn.

Skewer: A long thin metal or bamboo stick that is inserted through pieces of meat or vegetables to hold them together.

Slice: To cut food into thin, flat sections.

Sprinkle: A light dusting of seasoning, sugar, or flour. This is created when you hold the seasoning in your hand above the food at least 8 inches or so and rub your fingers together. It sprinkles down onto the food, almost like fairy dust!

Stir Fry: To use a wok or large skillet to cook food while stirring. The trick is to stir constantly, keeping the food moving in the pan until it is just tender.

Stir: To use a spoon or other utensil to move food around a bowl or pan. It helps combine ingredients, prevents sticking while cooking, and helps to cool food off after cooking.

Toss: To use two utensils or your hands to mix food together by gently lifting and then dropping it back into the bowl.

Whip: To use a wire whisk, electric mixer, or rotary beater to add air into a mixture.

Zest: The outer layer of citrus fruit, not including white membrane. This outer layer contains the fruit oils and is used as a seasoning. To get the zest from

a fruit, use a grater or fruit zester to scrape off the outer layer only.

Connect the dots to find out which Fun Foodie Friend this is!

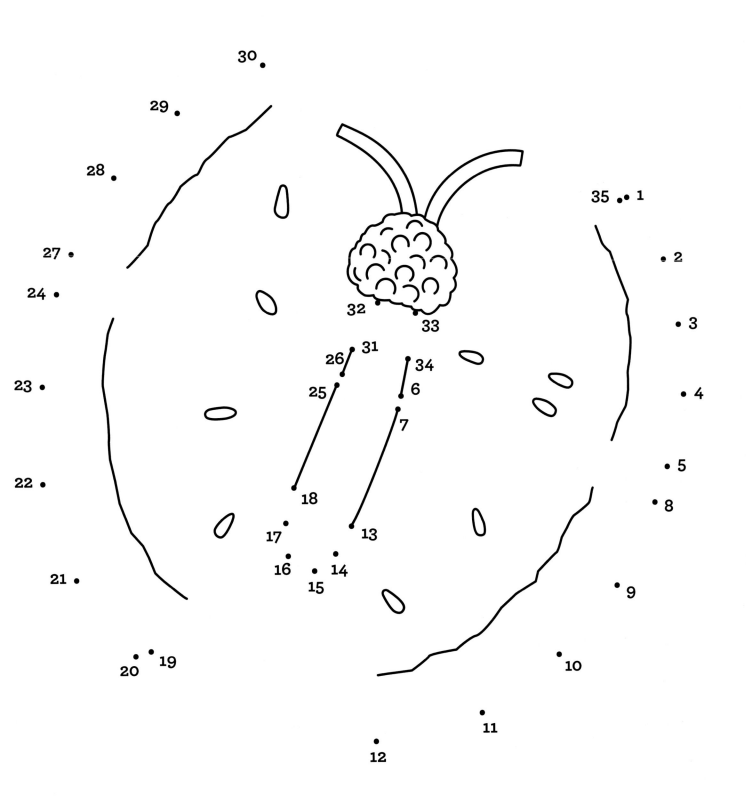

What foods do best friends Señor Guac and Señor Sammy have in common?

Circle all the foods that match.

Avocado
Cilantro
Carrot
Garlic
Green Pepper
Jalapeño Pepper
Kiwi
Lettuce
Lime
Pineapple
Potatoes
Red Onion
Tomatoes
Watermelon

Word Scramble Can you figure out the fruit and vegetable words below?

dacvoao ___ ___ ___ ___ ___ ___ ___

resubrelieb ___ ___ ___ ___ ___ ___ ___ ___ ___ ___ ___

toracrs ___ ___ ___ ___ ___ ___ ___

elcyre ___ ___ ___ ___ ___ ___

ubemuccr ___ ___ ___ ___ ___ ___ ___ ___

ñajpoael ___ ___ ___ ___ ___ ___ ___ ___

iikw ___ ___ ___ ___

teclute ___ ___ ___ ___ ___ ___ ___

ieml ___ ___ ___ ___

lpaipepne ___ ___ ___ ___ ___ ___ ___ ___ ___

emwtarleon ___ ___ ___ ___ ___ ___ ___ ___ ___ ___

WORD SCRAMBLE ANSWER: Avocado, Blueberries, Carrots, Celery, Cucumber, Jalapeño, Kiwi, Lettuce, Lime, Pineapple, Watermelon

SEÑOR GUAC AND SEÑOR SAMMY ANSWER: Jalapeño Pepper, Lime, Red Onion, Garlic, Tomatoes

Help Hoot-Hoot find his way to Leo Lion

Want to get to know your Fun Foodie Friends better? Write down some ideas of fun things you could do to learn more about them!

1. Visit a local farm.

2. Try a new food.

3. _____

4. _____

5. _____

6. _____

Start

Finish

COLOR Wheel

Artists use a color wheel to create colorful works of art.

Chefs use colorful fruits and vegetables to create yummy foods that are works of art!

Can you name the colors?

Can you name a fruit or vegetable of each color?

What is your favorite color?

____

What is your favorite fruit or vegetable?

____

Color: ______________________

Fruit or vegetable: ______________

____

Color: ______________________

Fruit or vegetable: ______________

____

Color: ______________________

Fruit or vegetable: ______________

____

Color: ______________________

Fruit or vegetable: ______________

____

Color: ______________________

Fruit or vegetable: ______________

____

Color: ______________________

Fruit or vegetable: ______________

____

COLOR ANSWER: Yellow, Orange, Red, Purple, Blue, Green

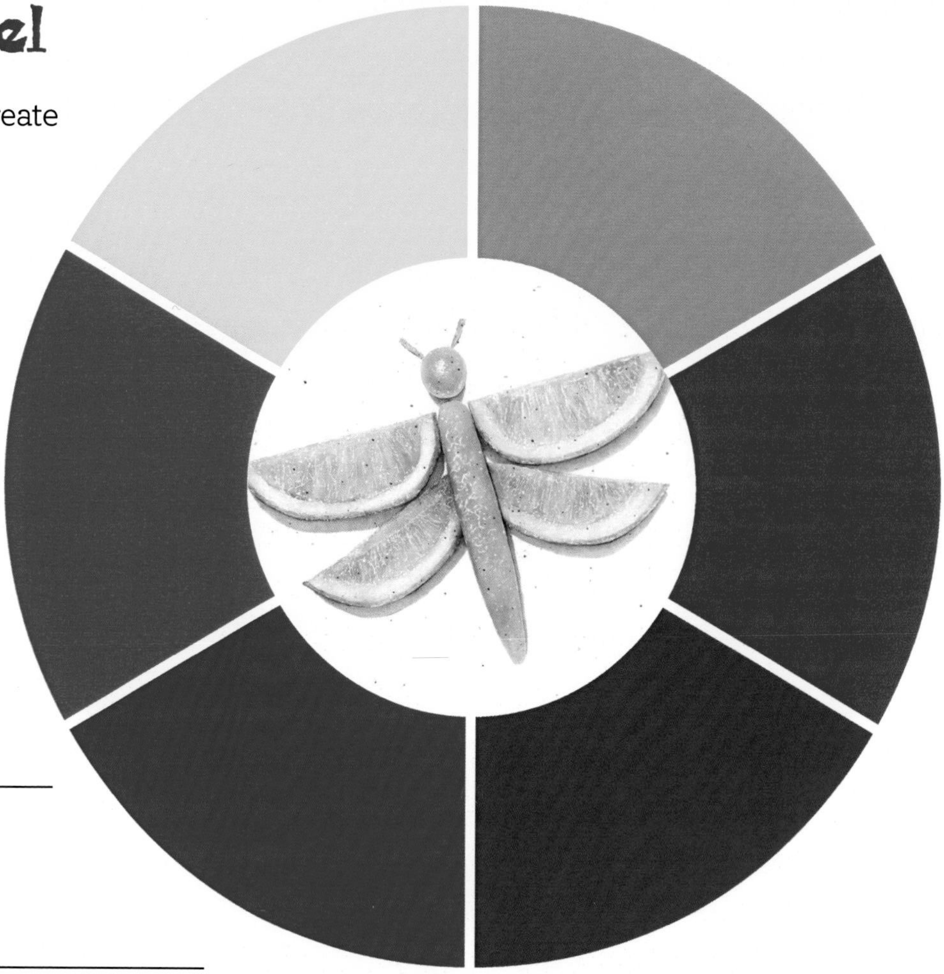

Party Pics to show off your food!

These Party Pics are the perfect way for Kid Chefs to show off their food creations. They're reversible and reusable. Carefully cut around the image on the dashed lines. Write your name on the Kid Chef line and place it with your food. Now everyone will know who the Kid Chef is!

CREATED BY
Kid Chef

CREATED BY
Kid Chef

CREATED BY
Kid Chef

CREATED BY
Kid Chef

CREATED BY
Kid Chef

CREATED BY
Kid Chef

More Party Pics to show off your food!

Here are more Party Pics for Kid Chefs to use to show off their food creations. They're reversible and reusable. Carefully cut around the image on the dashed lines. Write your name on the Kid Chef line and place it with your food. Now everyone will know who the Kid Chef is!

CREATED BY
Kid Chef

CREATED BY
Kid Chef

CREATED BY
Kid Chef

CREATED BY
Kid Chef

CREATED BY
Kid Chef

CREATED BY
Kid Chef